The mirror that won't talk, and your nightgown on the door,
The old pedal Singer just won't sing no more,
You can roll the reel for hours from the movie of this book,
It's a question mark on this heart of mine sends an elder back to look.
Chorus:-

Now I'm looking through a tunnel back into the room,
With the genius of a Druid when the sunlight floods the tomb,
And I'm never going back there, and I couldn't anyway,
'Cause though I made the great escape, I never got away.
Chorus:-

Connemara Girl

My Own Dear Galway Bay

Written by Frank Fahy (1845-1935), a native of Kinvara on the shores of Galway Bay.

Copyright Waltons Publications Ltd.

'Tis far a-way I am to-day from— scenes I— roamed, a boy.— And

long a-go the— hour I know I first saw Ill - in - ois.——— No

time, no tide nor— wa - ters wide could wean my heart— a - way.— For-

e - ver true I'll fly to— you, my— own dear— Gal - way Bay.

My chosen bride is by my side, her brown hair turning grey,
Her daughter Rose more like her grows from April dawn to day,
Our only boy, his mother's joy, his father's pride so gay.
With scenes like these I'd live at ease beside you, Galway Bay.

Oh, grey and bleak, by shore and creek, the rugged rocks abound,
But sweeter green the grass between than grows on Irish ground.
So friendship fond, all wealth beyond, and love that lives always.
Bless each dear home beside your foam, my dear old Galway Bay.

Had I youth's blood and hopeful mood and a heart of fire once more,
For all the gold this world could hold I'd never leave your shore.
I'd live content with whate'er God sent, with neighbours old and grey,
And I'd leave my bones 'neath churchyard stones beside you, Galway Bay.

The blessings of a poor old man be with you night and day,
The blessings of a poor old man whose heart will soon be clay.
There's one request I will ask of God upon my dying day:
Is my soul to soar forever more above you, Galway Bay?

Arthur McBride

This song was collected by Patrick Joyce around 1840. Joyce thought the song originated from Donegal. Like 'Mrs. McGrath' and 'The Kerry Recruit', it was written as an anti-recruiting song.

Arrangements copyright Waltons Publications Ltd.

He says, 'My young fellows, if you will enlist, a guinea you quickly shall have in your fist,
Besides a crown for to kick up the dust and drink the king's health in the morning.'
Had we been such fools as to take the advance, for the wee bit of money we'd have to
run chance,
For you'd think it no scruples for to send us to France, where we would be killed
in the morning.

He says, 'My young fellows, if I hear but one word I instantly now will out with my sword,
And into your bodies as strength will afford, so now my gay devils take warning.'
But Arthur and I, we took the odds, we gave them no chance to launch out their swords.
Our whacking shillelaghs came over their heads, and paid them right smart in the morning.

As for the young drummer, we rifled his pouch, and we made a football of his
rowdy-dow-dow,
And into the ocean to rock and to row, and barring the day it's returning.
As for the old rapier that hung by his side, we flung it as far as we could in the tide.
'To the devil I pit you,' says Arthur McBride, 'to temper your steel in the morning.'

Biddy Mulligan

This song, made famous by Dublin comedian Jimmy O'Dea, was written by
Seamus Kavanagh, author of many songs, including 'The Rose of Mooncoin'.

Copyright Waltons Publications Ltd.

I sell fish on a Friday spread out on a board,
The finest you'd find in the sea.
But the best is my herrings, fine Dublin Bay herrings,
There's herrings for dinner and tea.
I have a son Mick, he's great on the flute,
He plays in the Longford Street Band.
It would do your heart good to see him march out,
On a Sunday for Dollymount Strand.
Chorus:-

In the Park on a Sunday I cut quite a dash,
The neighbours look on with surprise.
With my Aberdeen shawlie thrown over my head,
I dazzle the sight of their eyes.
At Patrick Street corner for sixty-four years,
I've stood and no one can deny
That while I stood there, no one could dare,
To say black was the white of my eye.
Chorus:-

Fish and Vegetable Women

The Old Rustic Bridge by the Mill

Traditional

Arrangements copyright Waltons Publications Ltd.

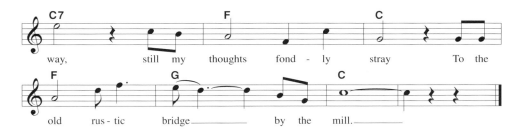

way, still my thoughts fond - ly stray To the

old rus - tic bridge by the mill.

I keep in my memory our love of the past,
With me it's as bright as of old.
For deep in my heart it was planted to last,
In absence it never grows cold.
I think of you darling, while lonely at night,
When all is peaceful and still.
My heart wanders back, in a dream of delight,
To the old rustic bridge by the mill.
Chorus:-

Rineen Mill, Co. Cork

The Spanish Lady

Traditional

Arrangements copyright Waltons Publications Ltd.

As I came back through Dublin City, at the hour of half past eight,
Who should I spy but the Spanish lady, brushing her hair in the broad daylight.
First she tossed it, then she brushed it, on her lap was a silver comb.
In all my life I ne'er did see a maid so fair since I did roam.
Chorus:-

As I went back through Dublin City, as the sun began to set,
Who should I spy but the Spanish lady, catching a moth in a golden net.
When she saw me, then she fled me, lifting her petticoat over her knee,
In all my life I ne'er did see a maid so shy as the Spanish Lady.
Chorus:-

I've wondered north and I've wandered south, through Stonybatter and Patrick's Close,
Up and around by the Glouster Diamond, and back by Napper Tandy's house.
Old age has laid her hand on me, cold as a fire of ashy coals.
In all my life I ne'er did see a maid so sweet as the Spanish Lady.
Chorus:-

The Valley of Knockanure

Written by Kerryman Brian McMahon, poet, author and school teacher, who died in 1997.

You may sing and speak a-bout Eas-ter Week and the he-roes of Nine-ty Eight, Of Fe - nian men who roamed the glen in vic - t'ry or de - feat. Their names on his-to-ry's pa - ges told, their me - m'ries will en - dure, Not a song was sung of our dar - ling sons in the Val - ley of Knock - a - nure.

There was Lyons and Walsh and the Dalton boy, they were young and in their prime,
They rambled to a lonely spot where the Black and Tans did hide.
The Republic bold they did uphold, tho' outlawed on the moor,
And side by side they fought and died, in the Valley of Knockanure.

It was on a neighbouring hillside we listened in hushed dismay,
In every house, in every town, a young girl knelt to pray.
They're closing in around them now, with rifle fire so sure,
And Lyons is dead and young Dalton's down, in the Valley of Knockanure.

But ere the guns could seal his fate, young Walsh had spoken thro',
With a prayer to God, he spurned the sod, as against the hill he flew.
The bullets tore his flesh in two, yet he cried with voice so sure,
'Revenge I'll get for my comrade's death, in the Valley of Knockanure.'

The summer sun is sinking low behind the field and lea,
The pale moonlight is shining bright far off beyond Tralee.
The dismal stars and the clouds afar are darkening o'er the moor,
And the banshee cried when young Dalton died, in the Valley of Knockanure.

I Never Will Marry

This 19th-century song concerns a woman who,
broken-hearted when abandoned by her lover, drowns herself.

Arrangements copyright Waltons Publications Ltd.

I ne-ver will mar - ry,____ I'll__ be no man's wife.____
____ I in-tend to stay sing - le____ for the rest of my life.____

One day as I rambled down by the sea shore,
The wind it did whistle, and the waters did roar.
I heard a poor maiden give a pitiful cry,
She sounded so lonesome at the waters nearby.
Chorus:-

'The shells in the ocean will be my deathbed,
And the fish in the water swim over my head.
My love's gone and left me, he's the one I adore,
I never will see him, no never, no more.'
She plunged her fair body in the water so deep,
She closed her pretty blue eyes, in the water to sleep.
Chorus:-

The Strand, Tramore, Co. Waterford

12

The Fish Carriers

The Little Skillet Pot

This song, popular in Ireland, first appeared in print in a 1947 American collection.

Arrangements copyright Waltons Publications Ltd.

Did you e - ver eat col - can - on made with love - ly pick - led cream? With the flour and sca - llions blen - ded like a pic - ture in a dream? Did you e - ver make a hole on top to hold the crea - my flake, Of the crea - my flav'-ry but - ter that my mo - ther used to make? Yes you did so you did, so did she and so did I, And the more I think a - bout it sure the near - er I'm to cry. Oh but were - n't they the hap - py days when trou - bles we knew not? And our mo - thers made col - can - non in the lit - tle skil - let pot.

Did you ever go a-courting as the evening sun went down,
And the moon began a-peeping from behind the Hill o' Down,
As you wandered down the boreen where the leprechaun was seen,
And you whispered loving phrases to your little fair colleen?
Chorus:-

Lough Sheelin Side

A plaintive ballad about emigration. Lough Sheelin is located just north of Mullingar, Co. Westmeath.

Arrangements copyright Waltons Publications Ltd.

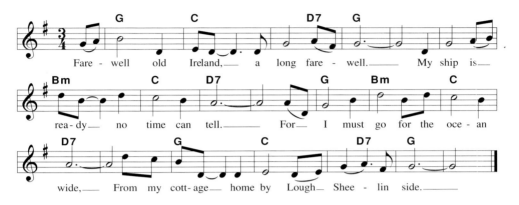

Fare - well old Ireland, a long fare - well. My ship is
rea - dy no time can tell. For I must go for the oce - an
wide, From my cott- age home by Lough Shee - lin side.

It was at the dance in the village green
I met young Eileen, my own cailín.
I took young Eileen, my fond young bride,
To my cottage home by Lough Sheelin side.

But our good dreams were too good to last,
The landlord came our home to blast.
And he no mercy on us did show,
As he turned us out in the blinding snow.

Will no one open to us a door,
In case that vengeance on them might fall?
'Twas there she fainted, 'twas there she died
As the snow fell fast by Lough Sheelin side.

They dug her grave in the churchyard low,
It was in the spring time when the daisies grow.
Sad tears were shed for my fond young bride
Who's sleeping now by Lough Sheelin side.

Farewell old Ireland and Eileen too,
My ship is ready, I bid adieu.
For I must leave for the ocean wide,
From my true love's grave by Lough Sheelin side.

Red Is the Rose

This simple love song shares the same air as the Scottish song, 'Loch Lomond'.

Arrangements copyright Waltons Publications Ltd.

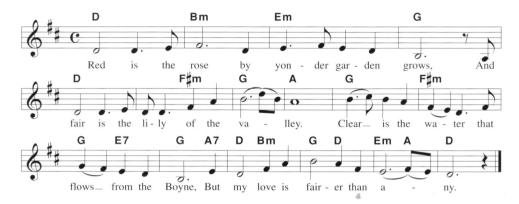

Red is the rose by yon - der gar - den grows, And
fair is the li - ly of the va - lley. Clear— is the wa - ter that
flows— from the Boyne, But my love is fair - er than a - ny.

Come over the hills, my bonnie Irish lass, come over the hills to your darling.
You choose the rose love, and I'll make the vow, and I'll be you true love forever.
Chorus:- (repeat after each verse)

'Twas down by Killarney's green woods that we strayed, And the moon and the stars they
were shining.
The moon shone its rays on her locks of golden hair, and she swore she'd be my love forever.

It's not for the parting that my sister pains, it's not for the grief of my mother.
It is all for the loss of my bonnie Irish lass, that my heart is breaking forever.

The Thatcher

The Merry Ploughboy

Traditional

Arrangements copyright Waltons Publications Ltd.

Oh I am a mer-ry plough-boy,— and I plough the fields all day,—

Till a sud-den thought came to my mind that I should run a - way.—

Well I'm sick and tired of slav-ery— since the day that I was born.—

So I'm off to join the I. R. A. and I'm off to - mor-row morn.—

Chorus

Well I'm off to Dub - lin in the green in the green where the

hel - mets glis - ten in the sun,— Where the bayo-nets flash, and the

rif - les crash to the ech - o of a Thomp-son gun.—

I'll leave aside my pick and spade, and I'll leave aside my plough.
I'll leave aside my old grey mare, for no more I'll need them now.
And I'll leave aside my Mary, she's the girl that I adore.
Well I wonder if she'll think of me, when she hears the cannons roar.
Chorus:-

And when this war is over, and dear old Ireland's free,
I'll take her to the church to wed, and a rebel's wife she'll be.
Chorus:-

The Raggle-Taggle Gypsy

This song, although popular in Ireland, is of Scottish origin. It tells of a lady, living in comfort and leisure, who absconds with the gypsies. The event is thought to have been an actual one.

Arrangements copyright Waltons Publications Ltd.

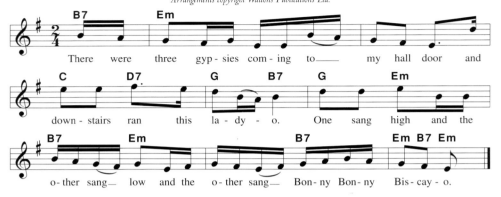

There were three gyp-sies com-ing to—— my hall door and down-stairs ran this la-dy-o. One sang high and the o-ther sang— low and the o-ther sang— Bon-ny Bon-ny Bis-cay-o.

Then she pulled off her silk-finished gown, and put on a hose of leather–o.
The ragged ragged rags about our door, she is gone with the raggle-taggle gypsy–o.

It was late last night when my lord came home, enquiring for his lady–o.
The servants said on every hand, 'She is gone with the raggle-taggle gypsy–o.'

'O saddle for me my milk-white steed, and go fetch me my pony–o,
That I may go and seek my bride, who is gone with the raggle-taggle gypsy–o.'

O he rode high and he rode low, he rode through wood and copses–o,
Until he came to a wide open field, and there he spied his lady–o.

'O what made you leave your house and land, what made you leave your money–o,
What made you leave your new-wedded lord, to be off with the raggle-taggle gypsy–o?'

'O what care I for my house and land, what care I for money–o?
What care I for my new-wedded lord, I'm off with the raggle-taggle gypsy–o.'

'Last night you slept on a goose-feathered bed, with the sheet turned down so bravely–o.
Tonight you'll sleep in a cold open field, along with the raggle-taggle gypsy–o.'

'O what care I for my goose-feathered bed, with the sheet turned down so bravely–o?
Tonight I will sleep in a cold open field, along with the raggle-taggle gypsy–o.'

The Leaving of Liverpool

This English ballad is also popular in Ireland. It is a song of lament at
having to emigrate to America and leave one's place of birth and loved ones.

Arrangements copyright Waltons Publications Ltd.

Fare - well to you my own true love, I am go-ing far far a-
way. I am bound for Ca - li - for-ni - a, And I know that I'll re-
turn some day. **Chorus** So fare thee well my own true love, For when
I re-turn un - it-ed we will be. It's not the leav-ing of Li ver-pool that
grieves me, But my darl-ing when I think of thee.

I have shipped on a Yankee sailing ship,
Davy Crockett is her name,
And her Captain's name was Burgess,
And they say that she's a floating hell.
Chorus:-

Oh the sun is on the harbour love,
And I wish I could remain,
For I know it will be a long, long time
Before I see you again.
Chorus:-

Mystic Lipstick

Words & Music by Jimmy MacCarthy

Copyright Jimmy MacCarthy (MCPS)

She wears mys-tic lip-stick, she wears stones and bones.

She tells myth and leg-end, she sings rock and roll.

She wears chains of bon - dage, she wears wings of hope.

She wears the gown of plen - ty, still it's hard to cope.

Chorus

'Chroí ó mo chroí your heart is break - ing. Your

eyes are red, your song is blue. Your

po - ets un - der-neath the will - ow in des-pair.

They have been lov - ers of your sad tune,

lov - ers of your slow air.

And tho' they fed on what hurts you,

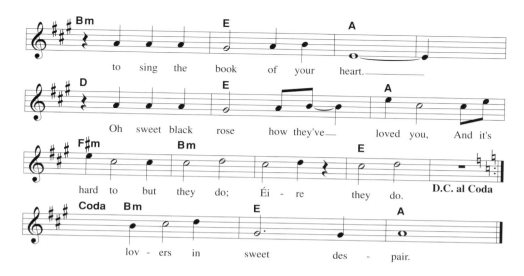

to sing the book of your heart.

Oh sweet black rose how they've— loved you, And it's

hard to but they do; Éi - re they do.

D.C. al Coda

Coda

lov - ers in sweet des - pair.

She keeps fools for counsel, she keeps the wigs and gown,
The cloth and bloody warfare, the stars, the stripes, and crown.
And still we pray for a better day now, God willing it's for the best,
But I've just seen the harp on the penny, with a dollar on her naked breast.
Chorus:-

A Charabanc (Touring Coach) Gougane Barra, Co. Cork

The Water Is Wide

Traditional

Arrangements copyright Waltons Publications Ltd.

The wa ter is— wide,——————— I can't— cross—
— o'er,—————— And nei- ther have I— wings to—
— fly.———— Give me a boat——————
———— that can car- ry two,—————————— And we shall
oar,————————— my love and I.——————

For love is gentle and love is kind, the sweetest flower when first it's new.
But love grows old and waxes cold, and fades away like the morning dew.

There is a ship, and she sails the sea, she's loaded deep, as deep can be,
But not as deep as the love I'm in, I know not how I sink or swim.

22

Whiskey in the Jar

This lively song, popular in Ireland, tells the story of a highwayman who
is betrayed by the woman he loves and subsequently taken prisoner.

Arrangements copyright Waltons Publications Ltd.

As I was go-ing o-ver the far famed Ker-ry Moun-tains, I met with Cap-tain
Far-rell and his mon-ey he was count-ing. I first pro-duced my pis-tol, and
then pro-duced my rap-ier, Say-ing stand and de-li-ver for you
are my bold de-cei-ver. With your whack fol the did-dle day.____ Whack for the
did-dle o,____ whack for the did-dle o, There's whis-key in the jar.

He counted out his money and it made a pretty penny,
I put it in my pocket and I gave it to my Jenny.
She sighed and she swore that she never would deceive me,
But the devil take the women for they never can be easy.
Chorus:- (repeat after each verse)

I went into my chamber all for to take a slumber,
I dreamt of gold and jewels and for sure it was no wonder.
But Jenny took my charges and filled them up with water,
And sent for Captain Farrell to be ready for the slaughter.

And 'twas early in the morning before I rose to travel,
The guards were all around me and likewise Captain Farrell.
I then produced my pistol, for she stole away my rapier,
But I couldn't shoot the water so a prisoner I was taken.

If anyone can aid me it's my brother in the army,
If I could learn his station in Cork or in Killarney.
And if he'd come and join me, we'd go rovin' in Kilkenny.
I swear he'd treat me fairer than me darling sporting Jenny.

23

The Homes of Donegal

Words & Music by Sean McBride

Copyright Waltons Publications Ltd.

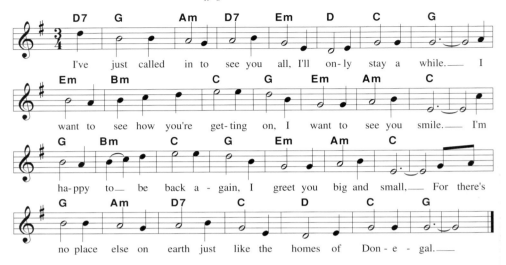

I've just called in to see you all, I'll on-ly stay a while.— I want to see how you're get-ting on, I want to see you smile.— I'm ha-ppy to— be back a-gain, I greet you big and small,— For there's no place else on earth just like the homes of Don-e-gal.—

I always see the happy faces, smiling at the door,
The kettle swinging on the crook, as I step up the floor.
And soon the taypot's fillin' up me cup that's far from small,
For your hearts are like your mountains, in the homes of Donegal.

To see your homes at parting day, of that I never tire,
And hear the porridge bubblin' in a big pot on the fire.
The lamp alight, the dresser bright, the big clock on the wall,
O, a sight serene, celestial scene, in the homes of Donegal.

I long to sit along with you and while away the night,
With tales of yore and fairy lore, beside your fires so bright,
And then to see prepared for me a shake-down by the wall.
There's repose for weary wanderers, in the homes of Donegal.

Outside the night winds shriek and howl, inside there's peace and calm,
A picture on the wall up there, our saviour with a lamp,
The hope of wandering sheep like me and all who rise and fall.
There's a touch of heavenly love around the homes of Donegal.

A tramp I am and a tramp I've been, a tramp I'll always be,
Me father tramped, me mother tramped, sure trampin's bred in me.
If some there are my ways disdain and won't have me at all,
Sure I'll always find a welcome in the homes of Donegal.

The time has come and I must go, I bid you all adieu,
The open highway calls me forth to do the things I do.
And when I'm trampin' far away I'll hear your voices call,
And please God I'll soon return unto the homes of Donegal.

A Fair Day at Glenties, Co. Donegal

The Galway Races

This song is a celebration of the annual horse racing event which
takes place in Galway on the west coast of Ireland.

Arrangements copyright Waltons Publications Ltd.

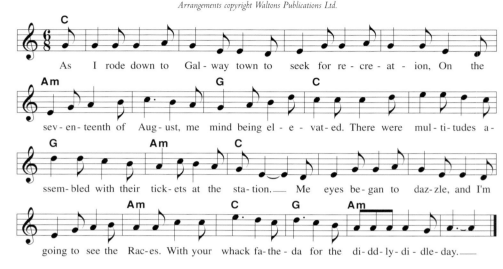

There were passengers from Limerick and more from Tipperary,
Boys from Connemara and a flair of married ladies,
People from Cork City who were loyal, true and faithful,
Who brought home the Fenian prisoners from dying in foreign nations.
With your whack-fa-the-da, for the diddly-diddle-day.

It's there you'll see the pipers and the fiddlers competing,
The nimble-footed dancers a-tripping over the daisies.
There were others crying cigars and likes and bills for all the races,
With the colours of the jockeys and the price and horses' ages.
With your whack-fa-the-da, for the diddly-diddle-day.

It's there you'll see the jockeys and they're mounted out so stately,
The pink, the blue, the orange and the green, the emblem of our Nation.
When the bell was rung for starting all the horses seemed impatient,
I thought they never stood on ground their speed was so amazing.
With your whack-fa-the-da, for the diddly-diddle-day.

There was half a million people there from all denominations,
The Catholic, the Protestant, the Jew and Presbyterian.
There was yet no animosity, no matter what persuasion,
But sportsman hospitality and induce fresh acquaintance.
With your whack-fa-the-da, for the diddly-diddle-day.

Home Boys Home

Traditional

Arrangements copyright Waltons Publications Ltd.

Oh when I was a young boy sure I longed to see the world,— To sail a-round the sea in ships and see the sails un-furled.— I went to seek my for-tune on the far side of the hill.— I've wand-ered far and wide— and of tra-vel I've had my fill.— And it's Home— Boys— Home, Home I'd like to be,— Home for a while— in the old coun-ter-y,— Where the oak and the ash and the bon-ny row-an tree— Are all grow-ing green-er in the old coun-ter-y.—

Well, I left my love behind me and I sailed across the tide,
I said that I'd be back again and take her for my bride.
But many years have passed and gone, and still I'm far away,
I know she is a fond true-love and waiting for the day.
Chorus:-

Now I've learned there's more to life than to wander and to roam,
Happiness and peace of mind can best be found at home.
For money can't buy happiness and money cannot bind,
So I'm going back tomorrow to the girl I left behind.
Chorus:-

Black Cave Tunnel, Larne, Co. Antrim

Roddy McCorley

This song was written by Eithne Carbury (1866-1902). Roddy McCorley, the son of
a miller, was executed after the 1798 Rising and buried beneath the gallows.

Arrangements copyright Waltons Publications Ltd.

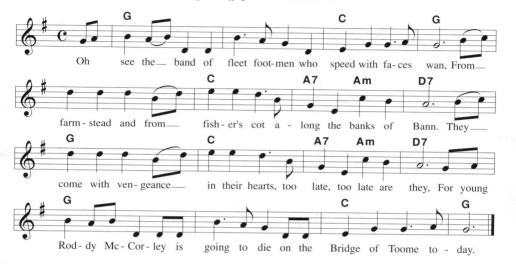

Oh see the band of fleet foot-men who speed with fa-ces wan, From
farm-stead and from fish-er's cot a - long the banks of Bann. They
come with ven-geance in their hearts, too late, too late are they, For young
Rod-dy Mc-Cor-ley is going to die on the Bridge of Toome to - day.

When he last stepped up that street, his shining pike in hand,
Behind him marched, in grim array, a stalwart earnest band.
For Antrim town, for Antrim town, he led them to the fray,
And young Roddy McCorley goes to die on the Bridge of Toome today.

Up the narrow streets he steps, smiling, proud and young,
About the hemp rope on his neck, the golden ringlets clung.
There was never a tear in his blue eyes, both sad and bright are they,
For young Roddy McCorley goes to die on the Bridge of Toome today.

Toomebridge, Co. Antrim

29

Sam Hall

This song, written by an Englishman, C. Ross, concerns a
chimney sweep who was hanged for burglary in 1701.

Arrangements copyright Waltons Publications Ltd.

Oh my name it is Sam Hall, chim-ney sweep, chim - ney sweep. Oh my
name it is Sam Hall, chim-ney sweep.——— Oh my name it is Sam Hall,—— and I've
robbed both great and small, and my neck will pay for all, when I
die, when I die. And my neck will pay for all, when I die.

Oh, they took me to Cootehill, in a cart, in a cart,
Oh, they took me to Cootehill in a cart.
Oh, they took me to Cootehill, and 'twas there I made my will,
For the best of friends must part, so must I, so must I,
For the best of friends must part, so must I.

Up the ladder I did grope, that's no joke, that's no joke,
Up the ladder I did grope, that's no joke.
Up the ladder I did grope, and the hangman pulled the rope,
And ne'er a word I spoke, tumbling down, tumbling down,
And ne'er a word I spoke, tumbling down.

Repeat first verse:-

The Patriot Game

Written by Dominick Behan brother of Brendan, it song tells the story of Fergus O'Hanlon
from Ballybay, Co. Monaghan, who was killed during the Brookborough attack at the age of 16.

Copyright Onward Music Ltd.

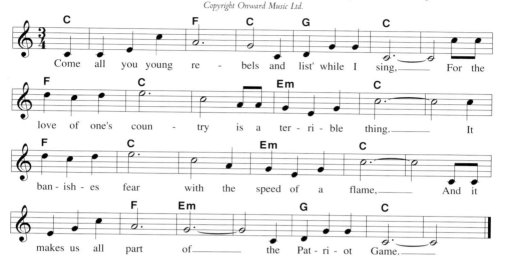

My name is O'Hanlon and I've just turned sixteen,
My home is in Monaghan where I was weaned.
I've learned all my life cruel England's to blame,
So now I am part of the Patriot Game.

It's nearly two years since I wandered away,
With the local battalion of the bold I.R.A.
For I read of our heroes and wanted the same,
To play my part in the Patriot Game.

They told me how Connolly was shot in a chair,
His wounds from the battle all bleeding and bare,
His fine body twisted, all battered and lame.
He died to be part of the Patriot Game.

The island of ours has long been half free,
Six counties are under John Bull's tyranny.
And yet De Valera is greatly to blame
For shirking his part in the Patriot Game.

Now as I lie here, my body all holes,
I think of those traitors who bargained and sold.
I wish that my rifle had given the same
To those quislings who sold out the Patriot Game.

Sixpence an Hour

The Irish Soldier Laddie

Written by Pat McGuigan, who also wrote, among other ballads, 'The Men Behind the Wire'.

Copyright Waltons Publications Ltd.

Said I to that soldier lad, 'Would you take me to your Captain?
It would be my pride and joy for to march with you today.
My young brother fell at Cork and my son at Enniscorthy.'
To the noble Captain I did say:
Chorus:-

As we marched back home again in the shadow of the evening,
With our banners flying low, to the memory of the dead,
Oh, we came back to our homes, but without our soldier laddie,
But I still can hear those brave words he said:
Chorus:-

Finnegan's Wake

The title of this well-known Dublin ballad was used by James Joyce for his famous book.

Arrangements copyright Waltons Publications Ltd.

Tim Finn-i-gan lived in Walk-er Street, a gen-tle Ir-ish man migh-ty odd. He'd a beau-ti-ful brogue so rich and sweet and to rise in the world he car-ried a hod. Now you see he'd a sort of a tipp-ling way with a love of liq-uor Tim was born, And to help him on his way each day he'd a drop of the creat-ur' ev'-ry morn.

Chorus

Whack for the hur-rah take your part-ners round the floor ye trott-ers shake. Is-n't it the truth I told you lots of fun at Fin-ni-gan's wake.

One morning Tim was rather full, his head felt heavy which made him shake.
He fell off the ladder and broke his skull, so they carried him home a corpse to wake.
They wrapped him up in a nice clean sheet, and laid him out upon the bed,
With plenty of candles around his feet and a couple of dozen around his head.
Chorus:-

His friends assembled at the wake, and Missus Finnegan called for lunch.
First they laid out tea and cakes, then pipes and tobacco and whiskey punch.
Then Biddy O'Brien began to cry, 'Such a lovely corpse did you ever see?
Arrah! Tim avourneen why did you die?' 'Ah! None of your gab,' said Biddy Magee.
Chorus:-

Then Peggy O'Connor took up the job, 'Arrah! Biddy,' says she, 'you're wrong I'm sure.'
But Biddy gave her a belt on the gob and left her sprawling on the floor.
Each side in war did soon engage, 'twas woman to woman and man to man.
Shillelagh-law was all the rage, and a row and a ruction soon began.
Chorus:-

Mickey Maloney raised his head, when a gallon of whiskey flew at him,
It missed and landed on the bed, the whiskey scattered over Tim.
Bedad he revives! See how he rises, Tim Finnegan jumping from the bed,
Crying while he ran around like blazes, 'Thundering blazes, ye think I'm dead!'
Chorus:-

Dominick Street, Mullingar, Co. Westmeath

The Harp that Once Through Tara's Halls

Written by Thomas Moore (1779-1852).

Arrangements copyright Waltons Publications Ltd.

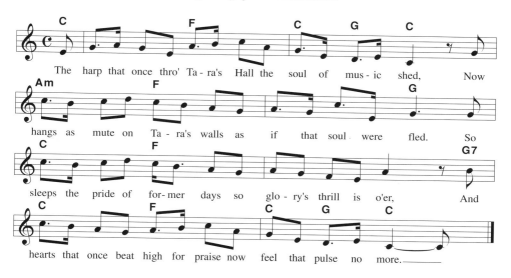

The harp that once thro' Ta-ra's Hall the soul of mus-ic shed, Now
hangs as mute on Ta-ra's walls as if that soul were fled. So
sleeps the pride of for-mer days so glo-ry's thrill is o'er, And
hearts that once beat high for praise now feel that pulse no more.

No more to chiefs and ladies bright the harp of Tara swells.
The chord alone that breaks at night its tale of ruin tells.
Thus freedom now so seldom wakes, the only throb she gives
Is when some heart indignant breaks, to show that still she lives.

Headfort Place, Kells, Co. Meath

The Banks of the Roses

This English folksong is simple, light and lively.

Arrangements copyright Waltons Publications Ltd.

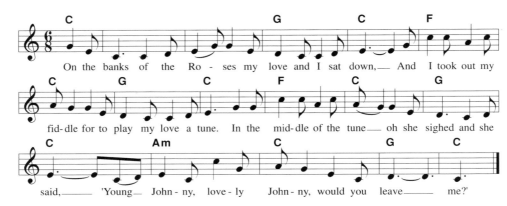

On the banks of the Ro - ses my love and I sat down, — And I took out my fid-dle for to play my love a tune. In the mid-dle of the tune — oh she sighed and she said, — 'Young — John - ny, love - ly John - ny, would you leave — me?'

When I was just a young lad, I heard my father say,
'I'd sooner see you dead and buried in the clay
Rather than be married, to any runaway
On the lovely sweet banks of the roses.'

Oh, well now I am a runaway and sure I'll let you know,
That I can take a bottle and drink with anyone.
And if her father doesn't like me, he can keep his daughter at home,
Then young Johnny will go roving with another.

If ever I get married, 'twill be in the month of May,
When the leaves they are green and the meadows they are gay.
And me and my true-love will sit and sport and play
By the lovely sweet banks of the roses.

The Foggy Dew

This song was written by Father P. O'Neill as a tribute to the men who
fought and died in the Easter Rising of 1916.

Arrangements copyright Waltons Publications Ltd.

Right proudly high in Dublin town they flung out the flag of war.
'Twas better to die 'neath an Irish sky than at Suvla or Sud El Bar.
And from the plains of Royal Meath strong men came hurrying through,
While Britannia's huns with their great big guns sailed in through the foggy dew.

O the night fell black and the rifles' crack made 'Perfidious Abion' reel,
'Mid the leaden hail, seven tongues of flame did shine o'er the lines of steel.
By each shining blade, a prayer was said that to Ireland her sons be true,
And when morning broke still the war flag shook out its fold in the foggy dew.

'Twas England bade our Wild Geese go that small nations might be free,
But their lonely graves are by Suvla's waves or the fringe of the Great North Sea.
O had they died by Pearse's side, or had fought with Cathal Brugha,
Their names we'd keep where the Fenians sleep, 'neath the shroud of the foggy dew.

But the bravest fell, and the requiem bell rang mournfully and clear,
For those who died that Eastertide in the springtime of the year.
While the world did gaze, with deep amaze, at those fearless men, but few,
Who bore the fight that Freedom's light might shine through the foggy dew.

Ah, back through the glen I rode again, and my heart with grief was sore,
For I parted then with valiant men whom I never shall see more.
But to and from in my dreams I go and I'd kneel and pray for you,
For slavery fled, O glorious dead, when you fell in the foggy dew.

Grafton Street, Dublin

Old Maid in a Garret

This lively ballad concerns a 45-year-old woman
who is not married and has never been asked.

Arrangements copyright Waltons Publications Ltd.

I have of-ten heard it said from my fa-ther and my mo-ther, That
go-ing to a wed-ding was the mak-ing of a-no-ther. Well if this be
so, then I'll go with-out a bid-ding. Oh—— kind prov-i-dence won't you
send me to a wed-ding? **Chorus** For it's oh dear me, how will it
be, if I die an old maid—— in a gar - ret?

Oh now there's my sister Jean, she's not handsome or good lookin',
Scarcely sixteen and a fella she was a courtin'.
Now she's twenty-four with a son and a daughter,
Here am I, forty-five, and I've never had an offer.
Chorus:- (repeat after every verse)

I can cook and I can sew, I can keep the house right tidy,
Rise up in the morning and get the breakfast ready.
But there's nothing in this wide world would make me half so cheery,
As a wee fat mannie who would call me his own dearie.

Oh come landsman or come kinsman, come tinker or come tailor,
Come fiddler or come dancer, come ploughman or come sailor,
Come rich man, come poor man, come fool or come witty,
Come any man at all who would marry me for pity.

Oh well I'm away home for there's nobody heeding,
There's nobody heeding, O poor Annie's pleading.
And I'm away home to me own we bit garret,
If I can't get a man, then I'll surely get a parrot.

41

The Three Flowers

This song, written by Norman G. Reddin, concerns the famous guerrilla fighter
Michael Dwyer, who lived in a cottage in the Glen of Imaal, in the Wicklow Mountains.

Copyright Waltons Publications Ltd.

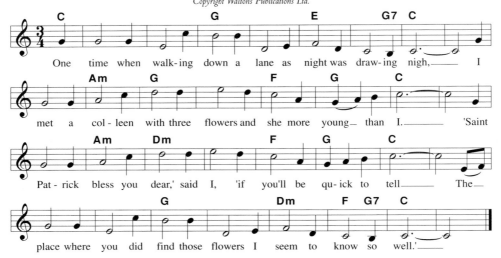

One time when walk-ing down a lane as night was draw-ing nigh,— I
met a col-leen with three flowers and she more young— than I.— 'Saint
Pat-rick bless you dear,' said I, 'if you'll be qu-ick to tell— The—
place where you did find those flowers I seem to know so well.'—

She took a flower and kissed it once, and softly said to me,
'This flower I found in Thomas Street, in Dublin fair,' said she.
'It's name is Robert Emmet, it's the youngest flower of all,
And I keep it fresh beside my breast, though all the world should fall.'

She took a flower and kissed it twice, and softly said to me,
'This flower comes from the Antrim Hills, outside Belfast,' said she.
'The name I call it is Wolfe Tone, the greatest flower of all,
And I'll keep it fresh beside my breast, though all the world should fall.'

She took a flower and kissed it thrice, and softly said to me,
'This flower comes from the Wicklow Hills, it's name is Dwyer,' said she,
'And Emmet, Tone and Dwyer, for I do love them all,
And I keep them fresh beside my breast, though all the world should fall.'

Only Our Rivers

This song was written by Michael MacConnell in 1973.

Copyright EMI. Music Publishing Ltd. Reproduced by kind permission of IMP Ltd.

When ap - ples still grow in No - vem-ber,—— When blos-soms still bloom from each tree,—— When leaves are still green in De - cem-ber,—— It's then that our land will be free.—— I've wand-ered her hills and her val-leys,— —— And still thro' my sor-row I see—— A— land that has ne ver known free - dom—— and on - ly her ri - vers run free.——

I drink to the death of her manhood,
Those men who'd rather have died
Than to live in cold chains of bondage,
To bring back their rights were denied.
Oh where are you now that we need you,
What burns where the flame used to be?
Are you gone like the snows of last winter,
And will only our rivers run free?

How sweet is life, but we're crying,
How mellow the wine, but we're dry.
How fragrant the rose, but it's dying,
How gentle the wind, but it sighs.
What good is in youth when it's ageing?
What joy is in eyes that can't see?
When there's sorrow in sunshine and flowers,
And still only our rivers run free.

Love Is Teasing

Traditional

Arrangements copyright Waltons Publications Ltd.

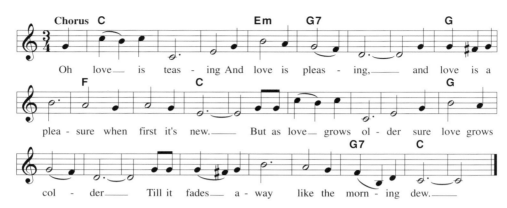

Oh love is teas - ing And love is pleas - ing, and love is a plea - sure when first it's new. But as love grows ol - der sure love grows col - der Till it fades a - way like the morn - ing dew.

I wish, I wish, I wish in vain,
I wish I was a maid again.
But a maid again I ne'er can be,
Till apples grow on an ivy tree.
Chorus:-

I left my father, I left my mother,
I left all my brothers and sisters too.
I left all my friends and my own relations,
I left them all for to follow you.
Chorus:-

But the sweetest apple is the soonest rotten,
And the hottest love is the soonest cold.
But what can't be cured, love, has to be
    endured, love,
So now I am bound for Amerikay.
Chorus:-

Mrs. McGrath

This was a popular marching song in Ireland during the years leading up to the
Easter Rebellion of 1916. Ironically it is a very evocative anti-war song.

Arrangements copyright Waltons Publications Ltd.

'Oh Mrs Mc-Grath,' the ser-geant said, 'would you like to make a sol-dier out of your son Ted? With a scar-let coat and a big tall hat, now Mrs Mc-Grath would-n't you like that?' With your too-ri-ay, fol the did-dle day, too-ri-you-ri roo-ri-ay.

Now Mrs. McGrath lived on the sea-shore, for the space of seven long years or more,
Till she saw a big ship sailing into the bay. 'Here's my son Ted, will ye clear the way.'
Chorus:-

'Oh, Captain dear, where have you been, have you been in the Mediteraneen?
Will you tell me the news of my son Ted, is the poor boy living or is he dead?'
Chorus:-

Ah well up comes Ted without any legs, and in their place he had two wooden pegs,
Well she kissed him a dozen times or two, saying, 'Glory be to God, sure it wouldn't be you!'
Chorus:-

'Oh then were ye drunk, or were ye blind, that ye left your two fine legs behind?
Or was it while walking on the sea, a big fish ate yer legs from the knees away?'
Chorus:-

'Well I wasn't drunk and I wasn't blind, when I left my two fine legs behind,
But a cannon ball, on the fifth of May, tore my two fine legs from the knees away.'
Chorus:-

'Oh Teddy me boy,' the old widow cried, 'yer two fine legs were yer mammy's pride.
Them stumps of a tree wouldn't do at all, why didn't you run from the big cannon ball?'
Chorus:-

'Well all foreign wars I do proclaim, between Don John and the King of Spain,
And by herrins I'll make them rue the time, that they swept the legs from a child of mine.'
Chorus:-

New York Girls
(Can't You Dance the Polka?)

Arrangements copyright Waltons Publications Ltd.

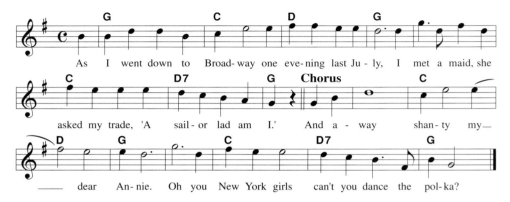

As I went down to Broad-way one eve-ning last Ju-ly, I met a maid, she asked my trade, 'A sail-or lad am I.' And a-way shan-ty my— —— dear An-nie. Oh you New York girls can't you dance the pol-ka?

To Tiffany's I took her, I did not mind expense.
I bought her a pair of gold earrings and they cost me 15 cents.
Chorus:-

She said, 'My fine new sailor, now take me home you may.'
But when we reached her cottage door she this to me did say:
Chorus:-

'My flash man he's a Yankee with hair cut short behind,
He wears a pair of tall sea boots and he sails in the black bow line.'
Chorus:-

'He's homeward bound this evening and with me he will stay,
So get a move on sailor boy, get cracking on your way.'
Chorus:-

I kissed her hard and proper before her flash man came,
Saying, 'Fare thee well me Bowery girl, I know your little game.'
Chorus:-

I wrapped me glad rags round me and to the docks did steer.
I'll never court another girl, I'll stick to rum and beer.
Chorus:-

I joined a Yankee blood boat and sailed away next morn'.
Don't mess around with women lads, you're safer round Cape Horn.
Chorus:-

The Galway Shawl

Shawls and cloaks were once worn by women throughout
Ireland. The style varied according to the locality.

Arrangements copyright Waltons Publications Ltd.

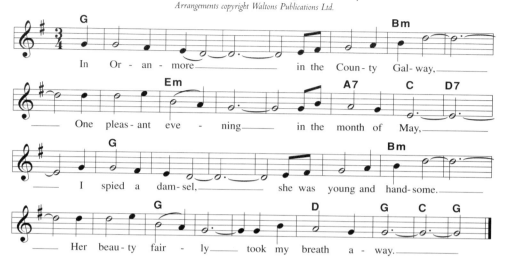

In Or - an - more in the Coun- ty Gal- way,
One pleas- ant eve - ning in the month of May,
I spied a dam- sel, she was young and hand- some.
Her beau- ty fair - ly took my breath a - way.

Chorus:
She wore no jewels or costly diamonds,
No paint or powder, no none at all.
She wore a bonnet, with a ribbon on it,
And around her shoulder was the Galway shawl.

As we kept on walking, she kept on talking,
Till her father's cottage came into view.
Said she, 'Come in Sir and meet my father,
And for to please him, play the Foggy Dew.'
Chorus:-

I played the 'Blackbird' and 'The Stack of Barley',
'Rodney's Glory' and 'The Foggy Dew'.
She sang each note like an Irish linnet,
And the tears flowed in her eyes of blue.
Chorus:-

'Twas early, early, in the morning,
I hit the road for old Donegal.
Said she, 'Goodbye Sir,' as she cried,
And my heart remained with the Galway shawl.
Chorus:-

The Queen of Connemara

Written by Frank Fahy (1845-1935) of Galway.

Copyright Waltons Publications Ltd.

When she's loaded down with fish till the water laps the gunwale,
Not a drop she'll take aboard her that would wash a fly away.
From the fleet she speeds out quickly like a greyhound from her kennel,
Till she lands her silvery store, the first on old Kinvara Quay.
Chorus:-

There's a light shines out afar and it keeps me from dismaying,
When the clouds are ink above us, and the sea runs white with foam.
In a cot in Connemara there's a wife and wee ones praying
To the one who walked the waters once to bring us safely home.
Chorus:-

Shop Street, Galway

Nora

The original lyrics were written by a Canadian, G.W. Johnston. The air is by J.A. Butterfield (1837-91).
Sean O'Casey changed the title from Maggie to Nora for his play, *The Plough and the Stars.*
Arrangements copyright Waltons Publications Ltd.

The vio - lets were scent-ing the woods, No-ra, dis - play-ing their
charms to the bees,—— When I first said I loved on - ly you,
No-ra, and you said you loved on - ly me.—— The chest-nut blooms
gleamed through the glade, No-ra, the rob - in sang out from ev' - ry
tree,—— When I first said I loved on - ly you,
No-ra, and you said you loved on - ly me.——

The golden-dewed daffodils shone, Nora,
And danced in the breeze on the lea,
When I first said I loved only you, Nora,
And you said you loved only me.

The birds in the trees sang their songs, Nora,
Of happier transports to be,
When I first said I loved only you, Nora,
And you said you loved only me.

Our hopes they have never come true, Nora,
Our dreams they were never to be,
Since I first said I loved only you, Nora,
And you said you loved only me.

The Jolly Beggarman

This song was probably written in the early 18th century. It tells the story of a beggar
who is given shelter by a farmer and subsequently seduces his daughter.

Arrangements copyright Waltons Publications Ltd.

He would not lie in the barn nor yet within the byre,
But he would in the corner lie down by the kitchen fire.
But then the beggar's bed was made of good clean sheets and hay,
And down beside the kitchen fire the jolly beggar lay.
Chorus:-

The farmer's daughter she got up to bolt the kitchen door,
And there she saw the beggar standing naked on the floor.
He took the daughter in his arms and to the bed he ran.
'Kind sir,' she says, 'be easy now, you'll waken my old man.'
Chorus:-

'Oh no, you are no beggar, you are some gentleman,
For you have stole my maidenhead and I am quite undone.'
'I am no lord, I am no squire, of beggars I be one,
And beggars they be robbers all, so you are quite undone.'
Chorus:-

She took the bed in both her hands and threw it at the wall,
Says, 'Go ye with the beggarman, my maidenhead and all!'
Chorus:-

When I Was Single

This English folk song, also called 'Still I Love Him', is said to have originated in East Anglia.

Arrangements copyright Waltons Publications Ltd.

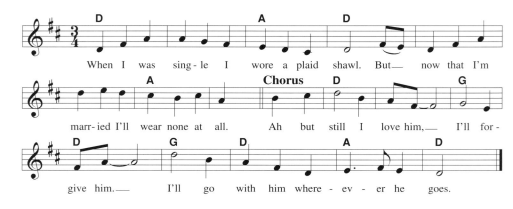

When I was sing-le I wore a plaid shawl. But— now that I'm marr-ied I'll wear none at all. Ah but still I love him,— I'll for-give him.— I'll go with him where - ev - er he goes.

Feeding the Chickens

He came up our alley
And he whistled me out,
But the tail of his shirt
From the trousers hung out.
Chorus:- (repeat after each verse)

He bought me a handkerchief,
Red, white and blue,
But before I could wear it
He tore it in two.

He brought me to an ale-house
And he bought me some stout,
But before I could drink it
He ordered me out.

He borrowed some money
To buy me a ring,
Then he and the jeweller
Went off on a fling.

There's cakes in the oven,
There's cheese on the shelf,
If you want any more
You can sing it yourself.

The Dying Rebel

Another song about the Easter Rising of 1916

Arrangements copyright Waltons Publications Ltd.

The night was dark,— and the fight was o-ver.— The moon shone down—

— O'Con-nell Street.— I stood a-lone,— where brave men per-ished.—

— Those men have gone— their— God to meet.—

My only son was shot in Dublin, fighting for his country bold.
He fought for Ireland and Ireland only, the harp, the shamrock, green, white and gold.

The first I met was a grey-haired father, searching for his only son.
I said, 'Old man, there's no use searching, for up to heaven your son has gone.'

The old man cried out broken-hearted, bending o'er I heard him say,
'I knew my son was too kind-hearted, I knew my son would never yield.'

The last I met was a dying rebel, bending low I heard him say,
'God bless my home in dear Cork City, God bless the cause for which I die.'

Patrick Street, Cork

Three Lovely Lassies

The suburb of Kimmage is located just south of Dublin city.

Arrangements copyright Waltons Publications Ltd.

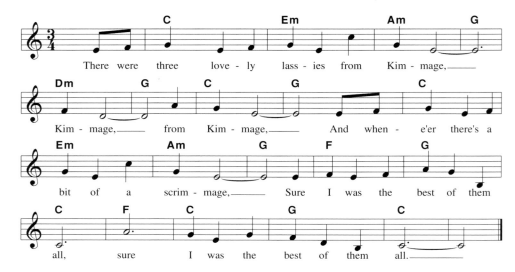

There were three love-ly lass-ies from Kim-mage,—— Kim-mage,—— from Kim-mage,—— And when-e'er there's a bit of a scrim-mage,—— Sure I was the best of them all, sure I was the best of them all.——

Well, the cause of the row is Joe Cashin, Joe Cashin, Joe Cashin,
For he told me he thought I looked smashin',
At a dance at the Adelaide Hall, at a dance at the Adelaide Hall.

He told me he thought we should marry, should marry, should marry.
He said it was foolish to tarry,
So he lent me the price of a ring, so he lent me the price of a ring.

When he gets a few jars he goes frantic, goes frantic, goes frantic.
Well he's tall and he's dark and romantic,
And I love him in spite of it all, and I love him in spite of it all.

Well me dad said he'd give us a present, a present, a present,
A stool and a lovely stuffed pheasant,
And a picture to hang on the wall, and a picture to hang on the wall.

I went down to the tenancy section, the section, the section.
The T.D. just before the election,
Said he'd get me a house near me ma, said he'd get me a house near me ma.

Well, I'm getting a house, the man said it, man said it, man said it,
When I've five or six kids to me credit,
In the meantime we'll live with me ma, in the meantime we'll live with me ma.

Take Me up to Monto

Montgomery St., Dublin – closed down in 1925 – was reputed to be the biggest red light district
of its kind, with an estimated 1600 prostitutes. The song was written by George Hodnett.

Arrangements copyright Waltons Publications Ltd.

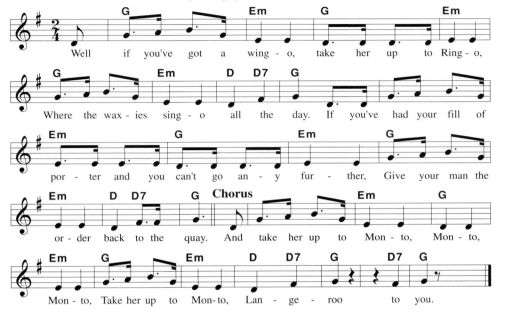

Well if you've got a wing - o, take her up to Ring - o,
Where the wax - ies sing - o all the day. If you've had your fill of
por - ter and you can't go an - y fur - ther, Give your man the
or - der back to the quay. And take her up to Mon - to, Mon - to,
Mon - to, Take her up to Mon-to, Lan - ge - roo to you.

You've heard of Butcher Foster, the dirty old imposter,
He took a mot and lost her up the Furry Glen.
He first put on his bowler, then he buttoned up his trousers,
And he whistled for a growler and he said, My men,
Take me up to Monto ....

The fairy told him, 'Skin the goat, 'O'Donnell put him on the boat,
He wished he'd never been afloat, the dirty skite.
It wasn't very sensible to tell on the Invincibles
They took aboard the principals, day and night.
Be goin' up to Monto ....

You've seen the Dublin Fusiliers, the dirty old bamboozaliers,
They went and got the childer, one, two, three.
Marchin' from the Linen Hall, there's one for every cannon ball
And Vicky's goin' to send youse all o'er the sea.
But first go up to Monto ....

When the Czar of Rooshia and the King of Prooshia
Landed in the Phoenix in a big balloon,
They asked the Garda Band to play 'The Wearin' o' the Green',
But the buggers in the depot didn't know the tune.
So they both went up to Monto ....

The Queen she came to call on us, she wanted to see all of us.
I'm glad she didn't fall on us, she's eighteen stone.
'Mr. Neill, Lord Mayor,' says she, 'is this all you've got to show to me?'
'Why no, ma'am there's some more to see – póg mo thóin.'

And he took her up to Monto, Monto, Monto,
Took her up to Monto, langeroo – Liathróidí to you.

Abercorn Street, Strabane, Co. Tyrone

The Flower of Sweet Strabane

This is one of the great Anglo-Irish love songs of the 19th century.

Arrangements copyright Waltons Publications Ltd.

If I were King— of Ire - land and all— things at my will,—— I'd roam through all cre - at - ion, new for - tunes to find still.—— And the for - tune I would seek the most— you all must un - der - stand,—— Is to win the heart— of Mar - tha, the Flow-er of sweet Stra - bane.——

Her cheeks they are a rosy red, her hair golden brown,
And o'er her lilly white shoulders it carelessly falls down.
She's one of the loveliest creatures of the whole creation planned,
And my heart is captivated by the Flower of sweet Strabane.

If I had you, lovely Martha, away in Innisowen,
Or in some lonesome valley in the wild woods of Tyrone,
I would use my whole endeavour and I'd try to work my plan
For to gain my prize and to feast my eyes on the Flower of sweet Strabane.

Oh, I'll go o'er the Lagan, down by the steam ships tall,
I'm sailing for Amerikay across the briny foam.
My boat is bound for Liverpool down by the Isle of Man,
So I'll say farewell, God bless you, my Flower of sweet Strabane.

Reilly's Daughter

This lively ballad deals with the pursuit of Reilly's daughter by
many a man who had to contend with a wild and dangerous father.

Arrangements copyright Waltons Publications Ltd.

As I was sit-ting by the fire, Eat-ing spuds and— drink-ing por-ter, Sud-den-ly a thought came in-to my mind. I'd like to mar-ry old Reil-ly's daugh-ter. **Chorus** Gid-dy I-ae, Gid-dy I-ae, Gid-dy I-ae for the one-eyed Reil-ly, Gid-dy I-ae, (Bang Bang Bang) play it on your old bass drum.

Reilly played on the big bass drum,
Reilly had a mind for murder and slaughter,
Reilly had a bright red glittering eye,
And he kept that eye on his lovely daughter.
Chorus:-

Her hair was black and her eyes were blue,
The colonel and the major and the captain sought her,
The sergeant and the private and the drummer-boy too,
But they never had a chance with Reilly's daughter.
Chorus:-

I got me a ring and a parson too,
Got me a 'scratch' in a married quarter,
Settled me down to a peaceful life,
Happy as a king with Reilly's daughter.
Chorus:-

I caught old Reilly by the hair,
Rammed his head in a pail of water,
Fired his pistols into the air,
A damned sight quicker than I married his daughter.
Chorus:-

The Snowy-Breasted Pearl

This air can be found in the *Collection* (1855) of George Petrie, who founded the Society for the
Preservation and Publication of the Melodies of Ireland. He lived at 67 Lower Rathmines Road, Dublin.

Arrangements copyright Waltons Publications Ltd.

Oh! thou blooming milk-white dove, to whom I've given my true love,
Do not ever thus reprove my constancy.
There are maidens would be mine, with wealth in land or kine,
If my heart would but incline to turn from thee.
But a kiss with welcome bland, and a touch of thy fair hand
Are all that I demand would'st thou not spurn.
For if not mine dear girl, oh! my snowy-breasted pearl
May I never from the fair with life return.

Brennan on the Moor

Brennan was a highwayman who robbed in Counties Cork and Tipperary and in the Kilworth
Mountains near the town of Fermoy. He was hanged in Cork sometime between 1804 and 1810.

Arrangements copyright Waltons Publications Ltd.

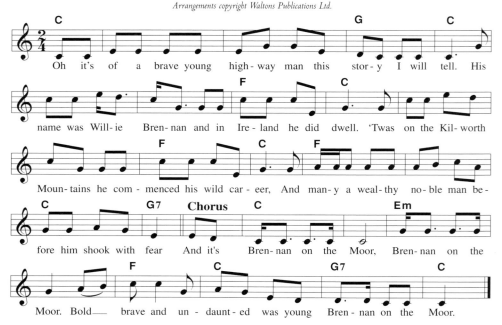

Oh it's of a brave young high-way man this stor-y I will tell. His
name was Will-ie Bren-nan and in Ire-land he did dwell. 'Twas on the Kil-worth
Moun-tains he com-menced his wild car-eer, And man-y a weal-thy no-ble man before him shook with fear And it's Bren-nan on the Moor, Bren-nan on the
Moor. Bold— brave and un-daunt-ed was young Bren-nan on the Moor.

Chorus

One day upon the highway, as Willie he went down,
He met the Mayor of Cashel, a mile outside the town.
The mayor, he knew his features, and he said, 'Young man,' said he,
'Your name is Willie Brennan, you must come along with me.'
Chorus:- (repeat after each verse)

Now Brennan's wife had gone to town, provisions for to buy,
And when she saw her Willie, she commenced to weep and cry.
She said, 'Hand to me that tenpenny,' as soon as Willie spoke,
She handed him a blunderbluss from underneath her cloak.

Then with this loaded blunderbuss, the truth I will unfold,
He made the Mayor to tremble and robbed him of his gold.
One hundred pounds was offered for his apprehension there,
So he with horse and saddle to the mountains did repair.

Now Brennan being an outlaw, upon the mountains high,
With cavalry and infantry to take him they did try.
He laughed at them with scorn, until at last 'twas said,
By a false-hearted woman he was cruelly betrayed.

Come to the Bower

This was a call to Irishmen abroad, but especially in America, to come back to
the home country to win our final freedom from oppression and tyranny.

Arrangements copyright Waltons Publications Ltd.

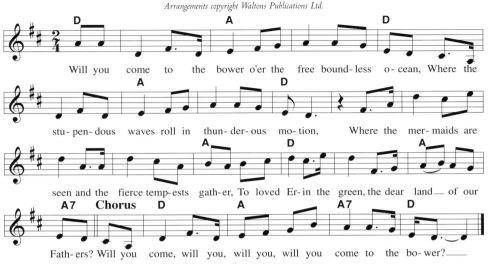

Will you come to the land of O'Neill and O'Donnell,
The patriot soldiers of Tirowen and Tirconnell,
Where Brian drove the Danes and St. Patrick the vermin,
And whose valleys remain still most beautiful and charming?
Chorus:-

You can visit Benburb and the storied Blackwater,
Where Owen Roe met Munroe and his chieftains of slaughter.
You may ride on the tide o'er the broad majestic Shannon,
You may sail round Lough Neagh and see storied Dungannon.
Chorus:-

You can visit New Ross, gallant Wexford and Gorey,
Where the green was last seen by proud Saxon and Tory,
Where the soil is sanctified by the blood of each true man,
Where they died satisfied, their enemies they would not run from.
Chorus:-

Will you come and awake our lost land from its slumbers,
And her fetters we will break, links that long are encumbered,
And the air will resound with Hosanna to greet you,
On the shores will be found gallant Irishmen to meet you.
Chorus:-

The Sash Me Father Wore

A song loved and sung by Orangemen in Northern Ireland.

Arrangements copyright Waltons Publications Ltd.

Sure— I'm an Ul-ster Or-ange-man, from— Er-in's Isle— I came,— To see my Glas-gow Breth - ren all of hon-our and of fame,— And to tell them of my fore-fath-ers who fought in days— of yore,— All on the twelfth day of Ju-ly in the sash me fath - er wore.—

Chorus:
It's ould but it's beautiful, it's the best you ever seen,
Been worn for more than ninety years in that little Isle of Green.
From my Orange and Purple Forefather, it descended with galore,
It's a terror to them Papish boys, the sash me father wore.

So here I am in Glasgow town, youse boys and girls to see,
And I hope that in good Orange style, you will welcome me.
A true blue blade that's just arrived, from that dear Ulster shore,
All on the twelfth day of July in the sash me father wore.
Chorus:-

And when I'm going to leave yeeze all, 'Good luck' to youse I'll say,
And as I cross the raging sea, my Orange flute I'll play.
Returning to my native town, to ould Belfast once more,
To be welcomed back by Orangemen in the sash me father wore.
Chorus:-

Believe Me If All Those Endearing Young Charms

This song was written by Thomas Moore (1779-1852). It was dedicated to his wife,
who on contracting a skin disease feared Moore would no longer love her.

Arrangements copyright Waltons Publications Ltd.

It is not while beauty and youth are thine own,
And thy cheeks unprofaned by a tear,
That the fervour and faith of a soul can be known,
To which time will but make thee more dear.
No, the heart that has truly loved never forgets
But as truly loves on to the close.
As the sunflower turns on her God when he sets
The same look which she turned when he rose.

The Boys of Fairhill

This song celebrates the victory of the junior Fairhill hurling team over the senior team in 1918.

Arrangements copyright Waltons Publications Ltd.

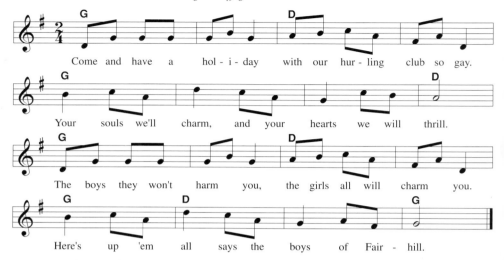

Come and have a hol - i - day with our hur - ling club so gay.

Your souls we'll charm, and your hearts we will thrill.

The boys they won't harm you, the girls all will charm you.

Here's up 'em all says the boys of Fair - hill.

Come on boys and you'll see lads and lassies full of glee,
Famous for all they will make your heart thrill.
The boys they won't harm you and the girls they will charm you.
Here's up 'em all says the boys of Fairhill,

Come on boys and spend a day with our Harrier Club so gay,
The loft of the bowl it will make your heart thrill,
When you hear the Shea boy say, 'Timmy Delaney won today.'
Here's up 'em all says the boys of Fairhill.

Now come on up to Fahy's Well for a pint of pure spring water,
The grandest place of all sure the angels do sing.
Thousands cross from o'er the foam, just to kiss the Blarney Stone,
Which can be viewed from the groves of Fairhill.

Come on down to Quinlan's pub, that is where you join our club,
Where 'round us in gallons the porter does flow.
First we'll tap the half a tierce and drink a health to Dashwood's rule,
That's the stuff to give 'em says the boys of Fairhill.

Now the stink on Patrick's Bridge is wicked, how does Father Matthew stick it?
Here's up 'em all says the boys of Fairhill.
Shandon Steeple stands up straight, the river Lee flows underneath.
Here's up 'em all says the boys of Fairhill.

Katty Barry sells crubeens, fairly bursting at the seams,
Here's up 'em all says the boys of Fairhill.
Christy Ring he hooked the ball, we hooked Christy, ball and all.
Here's up 'em all says the boys of Fairhill.